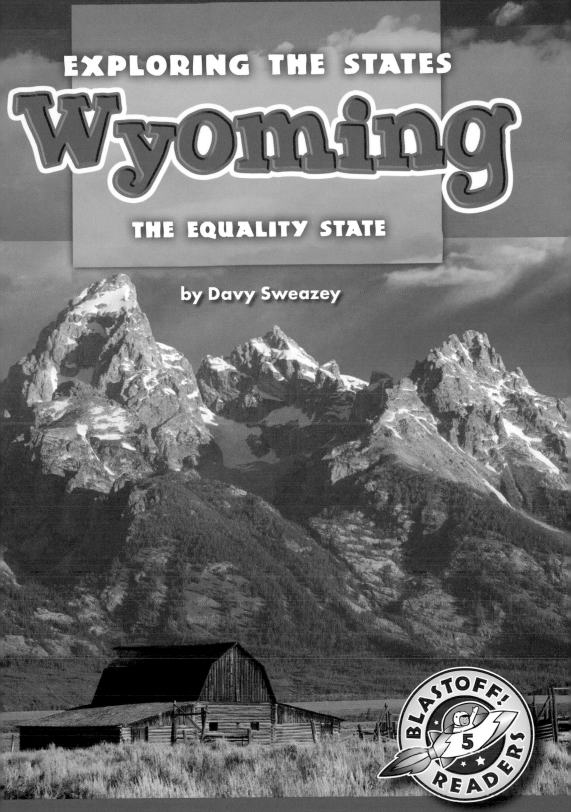

EXPLORING THE STATES

Wyoming

THE EQUALITY STATE

by Davy Sweazey

BELLWETHER MEDIA · MINNEAPOLIS, MN

Note to Librarians, Teachers, and Parents:

Blastoff! Readers are carefully developed by literacy experts and combine standards-based content with developmentally appropriate text.

Level 1 provides the most support through repetition of high-frequency words, light text, predictable sentence patterns, and strong visual support.

Level 2 offers early readers a bit more challenge through varied simple sentences, increased text load, and less repetition of high-frequency words.

Level 3 advances early-fluent readers toward fluency through increased text and concept load, less reliance on visuals, longer sentences, and more literary language.

Level 4 builds reading stamina by providing more text per page, increased use of punctuation, greater variation in sentence patterns, and increasingly challenging vocabulary.

Level 5 encourages children to move from "learning to read" to "reading to learn" by providing even more text, varied writing styles, and less familiar topics.

Whichever book is right for your reader, Blastoff! Readers are the perfect books to build confidence and encourage a love of reading that will last a lifetime!

This edition first published in 2014 by Bellwether Media, Inc.

No part of this publication may be reproduced in whole or in part without written permission of the publisher. For information regarding permission, write to Bellwether Media, Inc., Attention: Permissions Department, 5357 Penn Avenue South, Minneapolis, MN 55419.

Library of Congress Cataloging-in-Publication Data

Sweazey, Davy.
 Wyoming / by Davy Sweazey.
    pages cm. – (Blastoff! readers. Exploring the states)
 Includes bibliographical references and index.
 Summary: "Developed by literacy experts for students in grades three through seven, this book introduces young readers to the geography and culture of Wyoming"–Provided by publisher.
 ISBN 978-1-62617-051-3 (hardcover : alk. paper)
 1. Wyoming–Juvenile literature. I. Title.
 F761.3.S94 2014
 978.7–dc23
                                                                        2013014521

Table of Contents

Where Is Wyoming?	4
History	6
The Land	8
Yellowstone National Park	10
Wildlife	12
Landmarks	14
Cheyenne	16
Working	18
Playing	20
Food	22
Festivals	24
Rodeo	26
Fast Facts	28
Glossary	30
To Learn More	31
Index	32

Yellowstone
National Park

Idaho

N

W   E

S

Utah

Wyoming is a rectangular state in the northwestern
United States. It touches six other states. Montana sits on
the northern border. South Dakota and Nebraska lie to
the east. Colorado lines the southern edge. The state's
southwest corner cuts into Utah. Idaho shares the rest of
the western border.

Montana

South
Dakota

Gillette ●

Wyoming

Casper
●

Nebraska

Laramie ● **Cheyenne**
⭐

Colorado

Wyoming is one of eight
Mountain States. The Rocky
Mountains run through the western part of the state.
Wyoming's capital city, Cheyenne, sits at the foot of the
Laramie Range. It is located in the southeastern corner
of the state.

History

Native Americans were the first people to live in Wyoming. Their tribes included the Shoshone, Crow, and Sioux. European **trappers** and fur traders began coming to the area in the late 1700s. In 1803, the United States bought Wyoming land from France as part of the **Louisiana Purchase**. **Pioneers** traveled west through the state several decades later. Some stayed for cattle jobs. Wyoming became the forty-fourth state in 1890.

Native Americans in Wyoming

Wyoming Timeline!

1803: The United States gains land in Wyoming as part of the Louisiana Purchase.

1807: John Colter leaves the Lewis and Clark Expedition and explores Wyoming.

1825: The first major gathering for trappers takes place by the Green River.

1840s: Pioneers begin traveling through Wyoming on their way west.

1860-1861: Pony Express riders bring mail through Wyoming.

1872: The United States makes Yellowstone National Park the first national park.

1890: Wyoming becomes the forty-fourth state.

1924: Wyoming becomes the first state to elect a female governor, Nellie Tayloe Ross.

1988: Forest fires burn a large area in and near Yellowstone National Park.

fur trapping

Pony Express

Nellie Tayloe Ross

The Land

fun fact !

The Continental Divide follows the mountains of Wyoming on its way from Canada to Mexico. On the western side of the Divide, water flows west. Rivers and streams on the eastern side travel east.

The Rocky Mountains spread across much of Wyoming. These mountains divide into smaller ranges. **Basins** rest between the ranges. In the west, Gannett Peak reaches 13,804 feet (4,207 meters) into the sky in the Wind River Range. It is the highest mountain in Wyoming. In the southeast, the North Platte River circles the Laramie Range.

Wyoming's Climate

average °F

spring
Low: 31°
High: 56°

summer
Low: 51°
High: 82°

fall
Low: 32°
High: 58°

winter
Low: 14°
High: 36°

Snake River

Did you know?

Wyoming comes from a Native American word that means "land of vast plains."

The Green, Snake, and Yellowstone Rivers carry water from the mountains of Wyoming into larger rivers in other states. The **Great Plains** cover much of eastern Wyoming. Also in the east, the Black Hills stretch into Wyoming from South Dakota. The forested hills rise between the Belle Fourche and Cheyenne Rivers.

Yellowstone National Park

Grand Prismatic Spring

Yellowstone National Park fills the northwest corner of Wyoming and spills into Montana and Idaho. Set aside in 1872, it is the oldest national park. The Yellowstone River flows through the area. Its water rushes over waterfalls and between the colorful, rocky cliffs of the Grand **Canyon** of the Yellowstone. The canyon stretches for about 20 miles (32 kilometers).

Did you know?
More than half of the world's geysers are found in Yellowstone. The park has more than 300!

Old Faithful

The Rocky Mountains tower over Yellowstone National Park. **Geysers** and **hot springs** dot the landscape. Old Faithful is the most famous geyser. It sprays hot water 130 to 140 feet (40 to 43 meters) into the air. A variety of **minerals** and **algae** color the park's hot springs. At Mammoth Hot Springs, water washes gently over rocky **terraces**.

Wildlife

Herds of pronghorns roam through the sagebrush in Wyoming. Pronghorns are hoofed animals similar to antelope. Bison herds are found in the state's national parks. Their large size and raised backs make them easy to identify. White-tailed and mule deer graze on the flat land. Prairie dogs, gophers, and rabbits scurry on the ground at their feet.

Moose and elk wander on the hillsides. Bears and mountain lions prowl through the pine, spruce, and fir trees. Otters, beavers, ducks, and geese make their homes along the rivers, lakes, and streams. Bighorn sheep play on the rocks at the top of mountains. Bald and golden eagles soar above the rivers and trees.

fun fact !

Pronghorns are the fastest land animals in the western part of the world!

elk

pronghorn

bison

Devils Tower
National Monument

Did you know?
Thousands of people traveled through Wyoming in wagon trains on the Oregon Trail. The difficult journey from Missouri to Oregon took up to six months!

Wyoming is known for unique land features. Devils Tower National Monument is one of the most famous. The natural rock tower stands 867 feet (264 meters) tall. Fossil **Butte** National Monument is another popular **tourist** destination. The rocky ridges of Fossil Butte stick out and contain the **fossils** of many plants and animals.

Wyoming's greatest pride may be its national parks. Yellowstone and Grand Teton National Parks amaze visitors with mountain views and unique wildlife. In Cody, guests learn about the history and culture of the American West at the Buffalo Bill Center of the West.

fossilized bat

Grand Teton National Park

Cheyenne

Wyoming State Capitol

Cheyenne has a population of only about 60,000 people. The state capital is small compared to other cities in the U.S. However, it is big for the state with the fewest people. The city is named for a Native American tribe that lived nearby before settlers arrived.

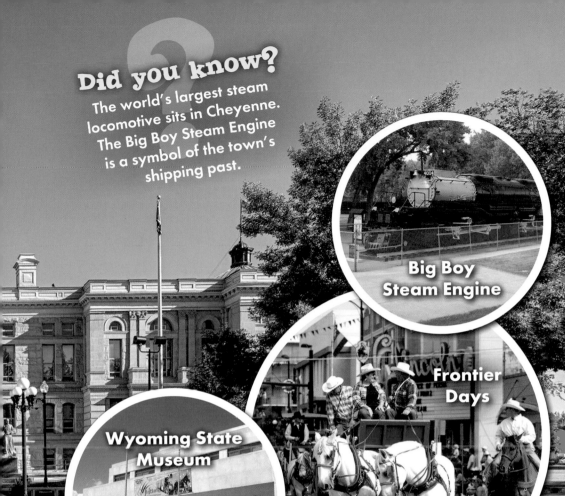

Big Boy Steam Engine

Frontier Days

Wyoming State Museum

An Old West history lives on in Cheyenne. Museums and a yearly celebration called Frontier Days remember the pioneers. Historic **Fort** D.A. Russell sits within Warren Air Force Base. During Fort D.A. Russell Days, actors in costumes bring this military fort back to life for visitors. At the Wyoming State Museum, visitors learn about the state's wildlife, **natural resources**, and history.

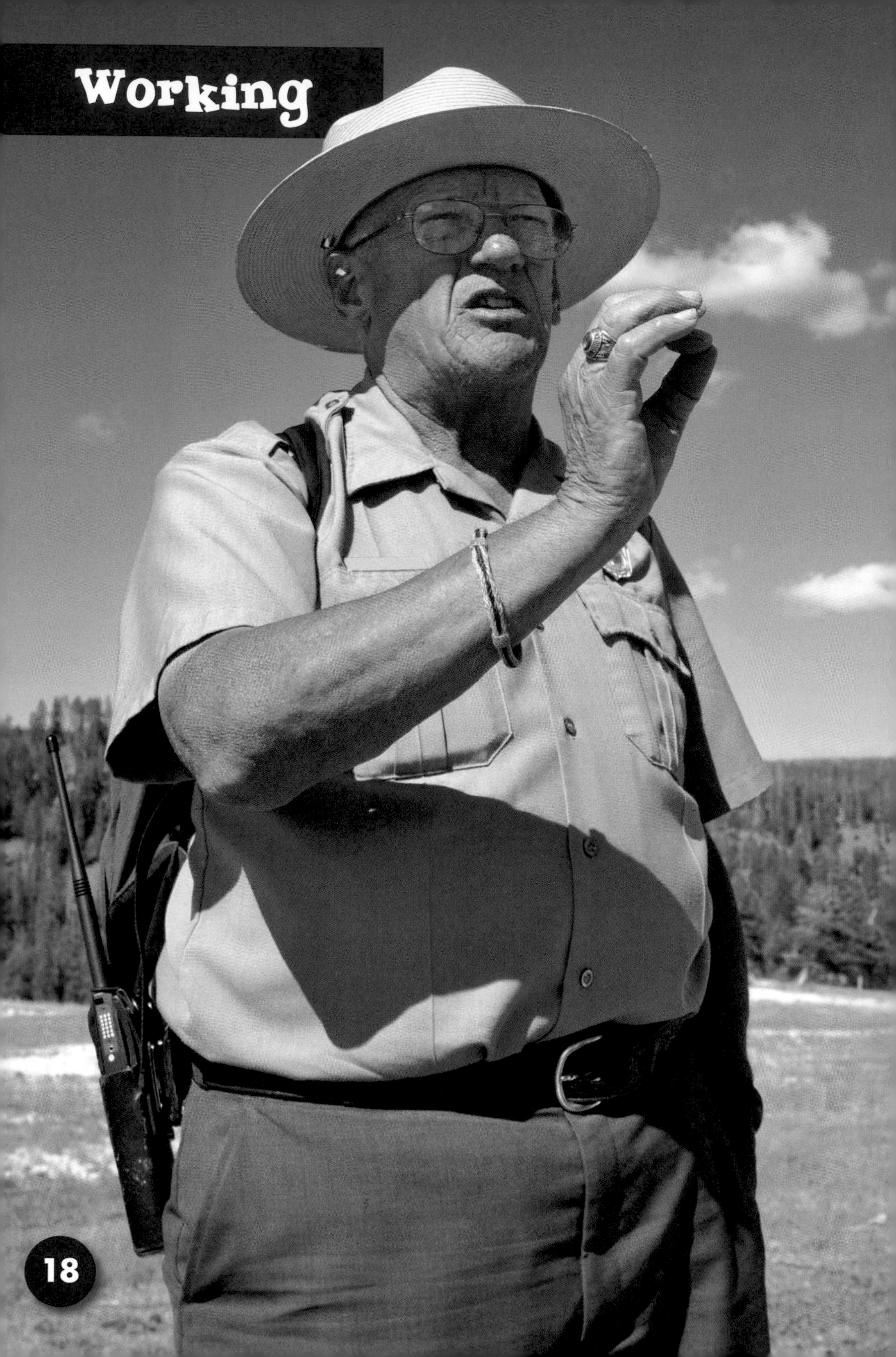

Service jobs employ a large number of Wyomingites. Federal government employees work at national parks and forests. Other employees work at Warren Air Force Base. Wyoming's natural beauty attracts tourists throughout the year. This means many people work at restaurants and hotels.

Many of Wyoming's jobs involve natural resources. Miners dig for minerals such as coal and uranium. Other workers process oil, natural gas, and a chemical called soda ash. Loggers cut down trees to make wood and paper products. Ranchers raise cows and sheep that graze on the grasslands. The animals provide important resources like meat and wool.

Where People Work in Wyoming

government
18%

manufacturing
3%

farming and
natural resources
12%

services
67%

Playing

Wyoming is a wonderland for nature lovers. The national parks and forests invite mountain climbers and hikers. Pronghorns and other large **game** animals keep hunters busy. Fishermen enjoy fly fishing in the rivers. During the winter, skiers and snowboarders from around the world travel to the Jackson Hole area. This valley is nestled deep in the Teton Mountains.

Wyoming does not have any major professional sports teams. Instead, Wyomingites cheer for the University of Wyoming in basketball and football. Community teams are also popular. **Rodeo** is a favorite sport in Wyoming. At a rodeo, cowboys and cowgirls compete in roping and riding competitions.

fly fishing

Kenny Sailors

fun fact

Kenny Sailors is one of the basketball players credited with the invention of the jump shot. He played for the University of Wyoming in the 1940s.

hiking

Food

chuckwagon dinner

Early Native American tribes in Wyoming ate what they could hunt, gather, or grow. They hunted animals like bison and elk and gathered berries and turnips. Some tribes grew corn and beans. Many of the tribes moved around in search of food.

Today people in Wyoming enjoy a variety of local meats. Restaurants serve bison burgers and steaks. Beef from cattle ranches is made into jerky, burgers, sausage, and more. Meat lovers also eat lamb, pork, and even goat meat. Some restaurants and ranches offer chuckwagon dinners. Food is served out of wagons like it was served on the trails to cowboys many years ago.

Milk Can Supper

Milk can suppers are a Wyoming tradition for feeding a crowd. Cowboys used 5-gallon or 10-gallon milk cans over an open fire to cook for a large group. If you don't have a milk can, a big, heavy pot on the stove will do just fine.

Ingredients:

4-6 cups of water

Per person:

1 Polish sausage, halved
1 potato, scrubbed
1 ear of corn, shucked
1/2 cup carrots, chopped
1/2 cup cabbage, chopped
1/2 cup onions, chopped

Directions:

1. Layer ingredients in the pot. Start with potatoes and water. Add carrots, cabbage, and onions. Then add corn. Sausages are the top layer.

2. Place the lid or a double layer of crimped aluminum foil loosely on top. Make sure there is room for steam to escape.

3. After 45 minutes, the pot should begin to steam. Let it steam for 45 more minutes. Have an adult carefully pour contents into a large serving tub.

4. Serve as a buffet with tongs.

For campfire cooking: Build a fire between 2 concrete blocks, with the milk can on the blocks. Keep the fire constant.

Festivals

Wyoming's major festivals celebrate the pioneers and mountain men of the past. Frontier Days has drawn people to Cheyenne every summer since 1897. In Old Frontier Town, guests step back in time with Buffalo Bill Cody and other characters. Native American dancing, food, and displays teach visitors about culture in Indian Village. Rodeo is the central event of Frontier Days.

In the 1820s, fur trappers and their suppliers began gathering together each year. They called the large gathering a **rendezvous**. Today, those meetings are remembered at mountain man rendezvous. Participants dress up in **buckskin** and other costumes from the time period. They build tepees and compete in shooting and archery. Other competitions include tossing a frying pan and throwing an ax.

fun fact !

Visitors to South Pass City can pan for gold during Gold Rush Days. They run water through a special pan of gravel and look for flakes of gold.

Frontier Days parade

Did you know?

Colorful rodeo clowns distract angry bulls to keep riders safe. Some also entertain the crowds.

rodeo clown

bronc riding

Cowboys and cowgirls rope and ride in Wyoming rodeos. Rodeo is the official state sport and has been popular since the late 1800s. The sport started as a cowboy tradition after long cattle drives. Cowboys would compete for the titles of best roper and best rider.

calf roping

Today, there are many more rodeo events. In bronc riding and bull riding, the rider's goal is to sit on a **bucking** horse or bull for eight seconds. The rider can only hold on with one hand. Cowgirls compete in barrel racing. They race on horses around three barrels and try not to knock the barrels down. Rodeos offer a thrilling glimpse into the culture of Wyoming and the American West.

27

Fast Facts About Wyoming

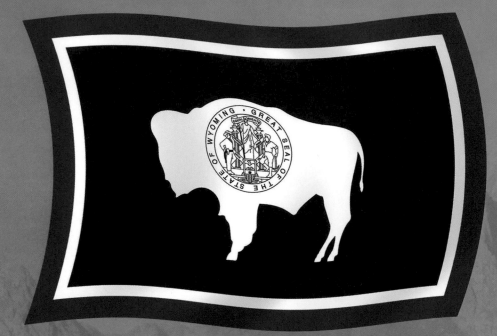

Wyoming's Flag

A bison stands in the center of a blue rectangle on Wyoming's flag. The state seal is located on the bison. A thin white border and a thick red border surround the rectangle. The blue stands for justice and the sky. The white stands for purity. The red stands for Native Americans and early settlers.

State Mammal
bison

State Nicknames:	The Equality State The Cowboy State
State Motto:	"Equal Rights"
Year of Statehood:	1890
Capital City:	Cheyenne
Other Major Cities:	Casper, Laramie, Gillette
Population:	563,626 (2010)
Area:	97,812 square miles (253,332 square kilometers); Wyoming is the 9th largest state.
Major Industries:	mining, ranching, services, tourism
Natural Resources:	oil, petroleum, coal, natural gas, uranium
State Government:	60 representatives; 30 senators
Federal Government:	1 representative; 2 senators
Electoral Votes:	3

State Bird
western meadowlark

State Flower
Indian paintbrush

Glossary

algae—plant-like organisms that grow in water or wet places

basins—areas of land that are lower than the surrounding land

bucking—jumping with an arched back

buckskin—soft leather clothing made from the skin of a deer

butte—a lone hill that rises out of flat land

canyon—a narrow river valley with steep, tall sides

fort—a strong building made to protect lands

fossils—the remains of plants and animals from the past that are preserved in rock

game—animals hunted for food or sport

geysers—springs that sometimes spray water into the air

Great Plains—a region of flat or gently rolling land in the central United States; the Great Plains stretch over about one-third of the country.

hot springs—areas where hot water flows up through cracks in the earth

Louisiana Purchase—a deal made between France and the United States; it gave the United States 828,000 square miles (2,144,510 square kilometers) of land west of the Mississippi River.

minerals—natural substances found in the earth

native—originally from a specific place

natural resources—materials in the earth that are taken out and used to make products or fuel

pioneers—people who are among the first to explore or settle in a place

rendezvous—planned gatherings

rodeo—an event where people compete at tasks such as bull riding and calf roping; cowboys once completed some of these tasks as part of their daily work.

service jobs—jobs that perform tasks for people or businesses

terraces—flat pieces of land that rise from the ground

tourist—a person who travels to visit another place

trappers—people who trapped animals to sell their fur

To Learn More

AT THE LIBRARY

Adkins, Jan. *What If You Met a Cowboy?* New York, N.Y.: Roaring Brook Press, 2013.

Gibbons, Gail. *Cowboys and Cowgirls: Yippee-Yay!* Boston, Mass.: Little, Brown, 2003.

Patent, Dorothy Hinshaw. *The Horse and the Plains Indians: A Powerful Partnership.* Boston, Mass.: Clarion Books, 2012.

ON THE WEB

Learning more about Wyoming is as easy as 1, 2, 3.

1. Go to www.factsurfer.com.

2. Enter "Wyoming" into the search box.

3. Click the "Surf" button and you will see a list of related Web sites.

With factsurfer.com, finding more information is just a click away.

Index

activities, 17, 20, 24

Big Boy Steam Engine, 17

Buffalo Bill Center of the West, 15

capital (see Cheyenne)

Cheyenne, 5, 16-17, 24

climate, 9

Devils Tower National Monument, 14, 15

festivals, 17, 24-25

food, 22-23, 24

Fort D.A. Russell, 17

Fossil Butte National Monument, 15

Frontier Days, 17, 24, 25

Gold Rush Days, 24

Grand Teton National Park, 15

history, 6-7, 14, 15, 17, 20, 22, 24, 26

landmarks, 10, 11, 14-15

landscape, 8-11

location, 4-5

mountain man rendezvous, 24

rodeos, 20, 24, 26-27

sports, 20, 26, 27

Warren Air Force Base, 17, 19

wildlife, 12-13, 15, 17

working, 6, 18-19

Wyoming State Museum, 17

Yellowstone National Park, 4, 7, 10-11, 15

The images in this book are reproduced through the courtesy of: Robcocquyt, front cover (bottom); Tomas Abad/ Age Fotostock/ SuperStock, p. 6; SuperStock, p. 7 (left); North Wind Picture Archives/ Alamy, p. 7 (middle); Associated Press/ AP Images, p. 7 (right); Dave Sucsy Photography, pp. 8-9; Lorcel, pp. 10-11; Lee Prince, pp. 11 (small), 12-13; Julie Lubick, p. 12 (top); Minden Pictures/ SuperStock, p. 12 (bottom); Bonish Photography, pp. 14-15; NHPA/ SuperStock, p. 15 (left); PdaMai, p. 15 (right); Nagel Photography, pp. 16-17; Andre Jenny/ Newscom, p. 17 (left); Luc Novovitch/ Alamy, pp. 17 (bottom), 24-25; Andre Jenny/ Alamy, p. 17 (top); Dennis MacDonald/ Age Fotostock/ SuperStock, p. 18; Inga Spence/ Alamy, p. 19 (small); Don Paulson Photography/ Purestock/ SuperStock, pp. 20-21; Kirk Strickland, p. 20 (top); Associated Press/ AP Images, p. 20 (bottom); Dmathies, p. 22; Emberiza, p. 22 (small); Anna Karwowska, p. 23 (small); Kathryn Sidenstricker, p. 24 (small); Margit Haegele/ Alamy, pp. 26-27; Phillip W. Kirkland, p. 26 (top); Nicholas J. Reid/ Getty Images, p. 26 (bottom); Trubach, p. 28 (top); Isselee, p. 28 (bottom); Ttphoto, p. 29 (left); Pictureguy, p. 29 (right).